Fun with Grammar

NOUNS

water boy

number

sea

pen

class

Samantha Green

Enslow Publishing
101 W. 23rd Street
Suite 240
New York, NY 10011
USA
enslow.com

Words to Know

capital The large version of a letter that appears at the start of sentences and names.

emotions The feelings people have inside.

general Involving a wide range of things that are not limited.

plural A type of word used to show that there is more than one of something.

pronoun A word that acts like a noun and describes another noun in the sentence.

specific Different and separate from other things.

Contents

WORDS TO KNOW 2

WHAT IS A NOUN? 5

PLACES 7

PEOPLE AND ANIMALS 9

THINGS 11

PROPER NOUNS 13

PRONOUNS 15

NOUNS AND ARTICLES 17

NOUNS YOU CAN'T SEE 19

COUNTING NOUNS 21

POWERFUL NOUNS 23

LEARN MORE 24

INDEX 24

The person holding this snowball is wearing gloves. *Glove* is also a noun.

What Is a Noun?

A noun is a person, place, or thing. Sometimes, nouns are things we can hold, like a snowball. Nouns are also things we can't hold, like happiness. *Happiness* and *snowball* are both nouns.

Planets make up the solar system.
Solar system **is another noun!**

Places

The names of places are nouns. Places can be big or small. Examples are *city* and *state*. Words like *bedroom* and *planet* are nouns, too! These nouns tell us where something is or where something happens.

Fast Fact

Nouns start many short sentences.

***Girl* is another noun that gives us information about Luisa.**

People and Animals

The names of people and animals are also nouns. The words *whale* and *ant* are both nouns. Nouns can give us information about people. *Teacher* is a noun, and so is *child*.

Fast Fact

Nouns can mean groups of people, like *firefighters*.

Pianos are made up of 88 keys. *Key* is a noun!

Things

The names of things are nouns. "Gregory wears his favorite socks when he plays the piano." *Piano* and *socks* are nouns that describe objects we can touch.

New York City is
famous for many
tall buildings.

Proper Nouns

Proper nouns describe things, people, and places that have names. They start with **capital** letters. "Ahmed lives in New York City." *Ahmed* is a person's name, and *New York City* is the name of a place. Both are proper nouns.

Goldfish is
also a noun.

Pronouns

Pronouns take the place of nouns. "Chen has a pet fish. Chen named the fish Sally." Using pronouns, we can say, "She named it Sally." *She* means Chen, and *it* takes the place of the word *fish*.

Fast Fact

Common pronouns are *she*, *his*, *them*, *it*, and *me*.

The letter *y* is sometimes called a vowel, too.

Nouns and Articles

Articles help us understand if a noun is **specific** or **general**. We use the article *the* before nouns we've already been talking about. *A* or *an* are articles we use for new nouns.

Fast Fact

When nouns start with a vowel (*a*, *e*, *i*, *o*, or *u*), use the article *an* instead of *a*.

“Leah should get a medal for her bravery.”

Nouns You Can't See

The names of things we can't touch are nouns, too. **Emotions**, such as *happiness*, are nouns, but the words used to describe our emotions are adjectives.

Fast Fact

For example, *bravery* is a noun, but *brave* is an adjective.

Count the number of puddles you can splash in!

Counting Nouns

Some nouns can be described with numbers. "After five thunderstorms, Ali was tired of bad weather." We can count *thunderstorms*. We can't count *weather*. But, both are nouns!

FAST FACT

Add an *–s* to the end of the noun to make it plural.

Without nouns, we wouldn't have words like *ball*, *water*, or *jacket*. Nouns are important!

Powerful Nouns

Our entire world is made up of nouns. The objects that we touch, the people we meet, and the places we go are all nouns.

Learn More

Books

Cossins, Jennifer. *101 Collective Nouns.* Sydney, Australia: Lothian Children's Books, 2019.

Dahl, Michael. *If You Were a Noun.* Minneapolis, MN: Picture Window Books, 2006.

Rosenthal, Betsy R. *An Ambush of Tigers: A Wild Gathering of Collective Nouns.* Minneapolis, MN: Millbrook Press, 2015.

Websites

Grammaropolis: The Nouns
www.grammaropolis.com/noun.php
Use quizzes, videos, and games to learn more about nouns.

Turtle Diary: Noun Games
www.turtlediary.com/games/noun.html
Play these noun games and see what you've learned about nouns!

Index

adjectives, 19
animals, 9
articles, 17
counting, 21
emotions, 19
general nouns, 17
names, 7, 9, 11, 13, 19
numbers, 21
people, 5, 9, 13, 23
places, 5, 7, 13, 23
plural, 21
pronouns, 15
proper nouns, 13
specific nouns, 9, 17
things, 5, 11, 13, 19
vowels, 17

Published in 2020 by Enslow Publishing, LLC.
101 W. 23rd Street, Suite 240, New York, NY 10011

Library of Congress Cataloging-in-Publication Data

Names: Green, Samantha, author.
Title: Nouns / Samantha Green.
Description: New York, NY : Enslow, 2020 | Series: Fun with grammar |
Includes bibliographical references and index. | Audience: Grades 1–4.
Identifiers: LCCN 2019009795 | ISBN 9781978512634 (library bound) | ISBN 9781978512610 (pbk.) | ISBN 9781978512627 (6 pack)
Subjects: LCSH: Grammar, Comparative and general—Noun—Juvenile literature.
Classification: LCC P271 .G74 2019 | DDC 415/.54—dc23
LC record available at https://lccn.loc.gov/2019009795

Printed in the United States of America

Photo Credits: Nouns – Photo research by Bruce Donnola

Cover, p. 1 Aaron Amat/Shutterstock.com; cover, p. 1 (pencil) OrangeVector/Shutterstock.com; p. 4 © iStockphoto.com/Ekaterina79; p. 6 © iStockphoto.com/rwarnick; p. 8 wavebreakmedia/Shutterstock.com; p. 10 © iStockphoto.com/Imgorthand; p. 12 © iStockphoto.com/Shooter_Sam; p. 14 © iStockphoto.com/Tom Merton; p. 16 Lim Yong Hian/Shutterstock.com; p. 18 © iStockphoto.com/Choreograph; p. 20 © iStockphoto.com/evgenyatamanenko; p. 22 2xSamara.com/Shutterstock.com; interior pages (notebook) Fascinadora/Shutterstock.com; interior pages (pencil) spacezerocom/Shutterstock.com